THE RIGHT DOG FOR THE JOB

Ira's Path from Service Dog to Guide Dog

Dorothy Hinshaw Patent

Photographs by William Muñoz

WALKER & COMPANY

NEW YORK

Thanks to the people at PawsAbilities and Guide Dogs for the Blind
for their help and cooperation on this project.
Special thanks to Sandy, KaDe, Don, Robbie, and Glenn.
—D. H. P. and W. M.

First published in the United States of America in 2004 by
Walker Publishing Company, Inc.

Published simultaneously in Canada by Fitzhenry and Whiteside, Markham, Ontario L3R 4T8

For information about permission to reproduce selections from
this book, write to Permissions, Walker & Company, 104 Fifth Avenue, New York, New York 10011

Library of Congress Cataloging-in-Publication Data

Patent, Dorothy Hinshaw.
The right dog for the job: Ira's path from service dog to guide dog / Dorothy Hinshaw Patent ; photographs by William Muñoz.
p. cm.
Summary: Tells how a golden retriever is trained as a service dog, to help someone who has trouble moving their arms or legs, and later as a guide dog for a man who cannot see.
ISBN 0-8027-8914-5 (HC) — ISBN 0-8027-8915-3 (Reinforced)
1. Guide dogs—Juvenile literature. [1. Guide dogs. 2. Golden retriever. 3. Dogs.] I. Title.

HV1780.P38 2004
362.4'183—dc22
2003065785

Book design by Victoria Allen

Visit Walker & Company's Web site at www.walkeryoungreaders.com

Printed in Hong Kong

2 4 6 8 10 9 7 5 3 1

Ira was born on Shy Bear Farm in Montana, along with his sister, Ivy, and his brother, Ike. Like all newborn puppies, the three young golden retrievers have closed eyes, velvety ears, and very soft fur. But unlike most puppies, these three were born for a special purpose. By the time they are two years old, each is expected to have become a service dog, helping a person who has difficulty moving around on his own to lead a fuller life. Ira, Ivy, and Ike are part of PawsAbilities, Canine Partners for People with Disabilities.

Ira's mother, Brea, with her puppies.

Photograph by Kathleen Decker

Kathleen holds onto the three wriggling puppies, with Ira in the middle.

Brea, the puppies' mother, and Kathleen Decker, PawsAbilities foster puppy coordinator, take good care of the puppies. They grow bigger and stronger. Their eyes and ears open so they can take in the world around them. Soon they are romping and playing together, getting bolder each day. Kathleen begins to feed them puppy food when they are four weeks old. By the age of six weeks, they no longer need their mother's milk. Soon it will be time to leave home.

Ira takes a
short break from
feeding time.

It's time to play!

Ira and Laddy play together.

Before they can help people with disabilities, service dogs need to learn to deal confidently with the world and whatever it might present to them—loud noises, smelly buses, crowds of people.

Each puppy goes to live with a special person called a foster puppy raiser. The puppy becomes a member of the family, where it gets plenty of love, attention, and praise as the puppy raiser introduces it to the world.

When they are about eight weeks old, Ira, Ivy, and Ike meet their puppy raisers. Ira goes home with Sandy Welch, a sixth-grade teacher in Lolo, Montana. Sandy already has her own beautiful golden retriever, Laddy Griz. Laddy and Ira quickly become friends. Kathleen visits Ira and Sandy a month later. She wants to see how Ira is doing and check on his service-dog skills.

Ira experiments with his food dish.

One of the most important tasks a service dog performs is retrieving things such as dropped keys. Sandy has already been working on this skill with Ira, so Kathleen throws her keys and tells Ira to fetch them. He runs over, picks them up in his mouth, and brings them back to Kathleen. Good news—Ira is already on his way to becoming a service dog!

Ira retrieves Kathleen's keys.

The puppies have fun playing together.

Photograph by Dorothy Hinshaw Patent

All along, the puppy raisers meet as a group to learn how to teach the young dogs what they need to know. The puppies have to learn how to come or to sit on command and how to walk at heel on a leash.

Kathleen also shows them how to teach the puppies to press a wheelchair-access sign with their paw. The symbol appears on buttons that open doors automatically when pressed. Kathleen uses a plastic lid attached to a stick with a strip of cloth. On the lid is the wheelchair-access sign. She puts a dog treat on the deck and covers it with the lid. One by one, the puppies sniff and push the lid with their noses, trying to get at the treat. But only when they scratch at it with a foot does Kathleen lift the stick so the puppy is rewarded.

Ivy tries to figure out how to get at the treat under the plastic lid.

Photograph by Dorothy Hinshaw Patent

**Ira gets
off the bus.**

The author sits with Ira and waits. Jim and Joan wait with their dogs, too. Just waiting is an important thing for a service dog to learn.

Next, the group goes to the bus station. The bus company loans PawsAbilities a bus and driver. The puppies practice getting on and off over and over again. They ride around town and learn to stay calm on the bus as it stops and starts. By the end of the day, riding the bus has become as natural as a trip in the car.

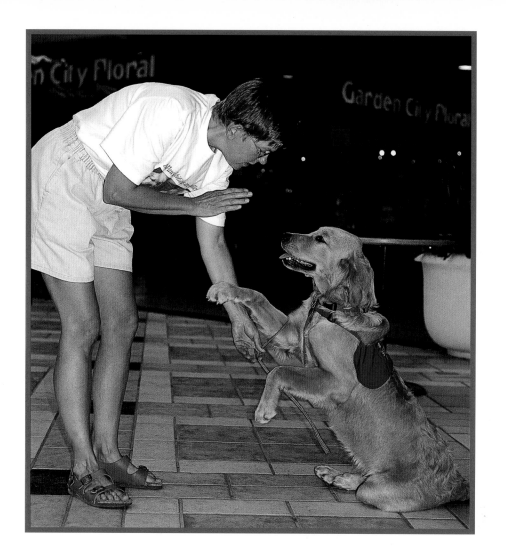

The puppy raisers take the dogs wherever they can, such as to sporting events and the farmers market. Every two weeks, the group meets at a different place somewhere in town. At the mall, the puppies learn not to be distracted at the pet store or by the crowds of people walking by. They also practice pushing the button with the wheelchair sign to open the door. At the university, they learn how to pull open a door using a tug made of rope tied to the knob. At the library, they learn to lie quietly under the table while the puppy raisers look through books. They also learn how to enter the elevator correctly, walking right beside the puppy raiser instead of going in front or behind. It would be dangerous if the elevator door closed on the leash.

Ira makes friends at the farmers market.

Photograph by
Dorothy Hinshaw Patent

Ira learns he must lie quietly for long periods of time.

Sandy brings Ira to her classroom two days a week. She explains to her students the importance of training Ira correctly.

"Ira needs to learn to lie down by himself and stay there, even if he gets bored," she says. "You have to leave him alone, even if he wants to be petted,

so he doesn't get distracted from his job. You can also help teach the other children not to pet a service dog in training."

Ira has his own corner of the room, where he must lie quietly on his rug. If he gets up and wanders around, Sandy says in a firm voice, "Rug!" Then she tells Ira to sit, lie down, or stay. He must also learn to always stay close to the person he is helping.

Each week, one student has the job of giving Ira water, brushing his coat, and walking him.

Ira learns to come when he is called.

It takes lots of practice for Ira to learn to flip a light switch with his nose instead of his mouth.

When Sandy and the students work with Ira, they form a circle and bring Ira into the center. Then one of the children calls him. He knows he'll get a treat if he lays his head in the child's lap. The children take turns calling him, helping him learn to come reliably every time he is called. Then they help teach him to use his nose to push a light switch, another important job for a service dog to learn.

Ira goes all over the school, so he gets used to noisy places like the cafeteria and the gym during pep rallies. Sandy also takes him to other classrooms and tells the other students about service dogs.

Stephanie plays with a puppy.

Jeremy cuddles with a new friend.

As summer approaches, Sandy's students must say good-bye to Ira. Each child gets a chance to say what having Ira in the classroom meant to her or him.

"I feel special because I got to help train Ira," says one.

"I never liked dogs before Ira came, but now I like having him around," confesses another.

"Having Ira in the classroom has made me feel beyond wonderful," says a third.

Ember says good-bye to Ira.

To reward the children for their help, Sandy arranges a field trip to Shy Bear Farm. The students take turns making dog toys, working on scrapbooks for Ira's new companion, touring the farm, and playing with the six-week-old puppies. They also get to say one last good-bye to Ira.

Puppies at play at Guide Dogs for the Blind.

As summer starts it's time for Ira to leave Sandy and go for more detailed service-dog training. But his assigned training facility isn't ready yet. Glenn Martyn, director of PawsAbilities, can't find another service-dog group that can use Ira. Everyone worries. What will happen? Can Ira learn a new career?

Though they rarely take dogs raised and trained elsewhere, Guide Dogs for the Blind in San Rafael, California, steps in. "Ira has lots of confidence, which is very important in a guide dog, so we'll give Ira a chance," says their coordinator. "But we'll have to change his name. Each dog we train has a different name, and we already have one called Ira. We'll just change the spelling to 'Irah' so he won't have to learn a new name."

Guide Dogs for the Blind uses more Labrador retrievers than golden retrievers.

Puppy socializers get the young dogs used to handling from an early age.

Stacy works Irah on the Guide Dogs for the Blind campus.

Photograph by
Dorothy Hinshaw Patent

Now Irah needs to learn a whole new set of skills, which takes four to five months. He has to get used to wearing a guide-dog harness. Trainer Stacy Burrow helps him learn many things, such as stopping at street corners and crossing only when the way is clear.

The most important thing a guide dog must learn is intelligent disobedience. Knowing when to disobey can enable a guide dog to save its owner's life. For example, if the blind person tells the dog to go forward when a car is running a red light, the dog must refuse to obey. Irah is smart. He passes the program with flying colors.

Irah learns when it's safe to cross the street.

Photograph by
Dorothy Hinshaw Patent

With head trainer Mike Del Ross looking on, Irah and Don show how well they work together.

With Don in the background, Sandy and Irah greet one another at Guide Dogs for the Blind.

After training, Irah is paired with Don Simmonson, a piano tuner who had already retired two guide dogs after they got too old to work. Irah and Don work together for three weeks in San Rafael, learning to be a team. Then it's time to graduate.

Sandy comes from Montana for the graduation. She gets to see Irah and meet Don before the ceremony. Irah and Sandy are delighted to be together again, but Irah clearly knows his place is now with Don.

During the graduation ceremony, Don's name is announced when his turn comes. Sandy hands Irah over to Don. Irah is Don's dog now, and the two will be loving, giving partners. Sandy will miss Irah, but she is happy that he has found a home with someone like Don.

Stacy, Sandy, and Irah stand by as Don speaks at the graduation.

Irah and Grayson enjoy playing together.

At home in Kennewick, Washington, Don and Irah continue to learn to work together. Grayson, Don's retired guide dog, also lives with them. Grayson and Irah become fast friends, playing together just like Irah and Laddy did.

When Don goes to work, Irah guides him. Once they enter the room with the piano, Don says, "Irah, find the piano," and Irah leads him to it. Then Don gets to work and Irah lies down nearby, waiting patiently, as he learned to do in Sandy's classroom. He is there for Don whenever he is needed.

"I'm so glad Irah and I found each other," Don says. "He's just the right dog for me."

Irah waits
patiently while
Don works.

rah guides Don
n Kennewick.

Two years after she said good-bye to Irah, Ember is happy to say hello again.

Photograph by
Dorothy Hinshaw Patent

Sandy and Don become friends, and, as a surprise, Sandy invites Don to the eighth-grade graduation of the children who helped train Irah.

Don's wife, Robbie, drives their motor home to Montana for the graduation. After Sandy talks to the audience about Irah and Don, she shows a movie of their graduation from Guide Dogs for the Blind. Then she announces that Don and Irah are in the auditorium, and Joey, Irah's favorite student, escorts them to the stage. The surprised students are delighted to see the results of their hard work and the hard work of so many others. Their own canine student, Irah, is now a working guide dog!

Joey escorts Don and Irah to the stage for their big moment.

Photograph by
Kurt Wilson

Across the country there are many organizations that provide service dogs and guide dogs for people. Generally, such organizations recruit puppy raisers to love and care for their dogs when young and expose them to all sorts of environments so they will become confident, capable, and loving animals. If you want to get involved, here are a few organizations to contact:

Canine Companions for Independence provides assistance dogs for people across the United States. The home office is in Santa Rosa, California, but the organization also has branches in Orlando, Florida; Delaware, Ohio; Oceanside, California; Farmingdale, New York; and Colorado Springs, Colorado.

Canine Companions for Independence
2965 Dutton Avenue
P.O. Box 446
Santa Rosa, CA 95402-0446
(707) 577-1700 Voice
(707) 577-1756 TDD
info@caninecompanions.org
www.caninecompanions.org

The Delta Society works with all sorts of organizations that provide helping animals.

The Delta Society
580 Naches Avenue S.W.
Suite 101
Renton, WA 98055-2297
(425) 226-7357

Guide Dogs for the Blind
P.O. Box 151200
San Rafael, CA 94915
(800) 295-4050
www.guidedogs.com

Guide Dogs also has a campus in Oregon:

Guide Dogs for the Blind
32901 S.E. Kelso Road
Boring, OR 97009
(503) 668-2100

Guiding Eyes for the Blind
611 Granite Springs Road
Yorktown Heights, NY 10598
(800) 942-0149
info@guidingeyes.org

PawsAbilities
Kathleen Decker
320 Shy Bear Farm Road
Arlee, MT 59821
(406) 726-4149

The Seeing Eye
P.O. Box 375
Morristown, NJ 07963-0375
(800) 539-4425
www.seeingeye.org

For Further Reading

Lang, Glenna. *Looking Out for Sarah*. Watertown, MA: Talewinds, 2001.

Lawrenson, Diana. *Guide Dogs: From Puppies to Partners*. Sydney: Allen and Unwin, 2002.

Moore, Eva, and Don Bolognese. *Buddy: The First Seeing Eye Dog*. New York: Cartwheel Books, 1996.

Osofsky, Audrey, and Ted Rand. *My Buddy*. New York: Henry Holt, 1992.

Rossiter, Nan Parson. *Rugby & Rosie*. New York: Dutton, 1997.